Two Squirrels and a Mouse

A Christmas Story

Jack DiNola

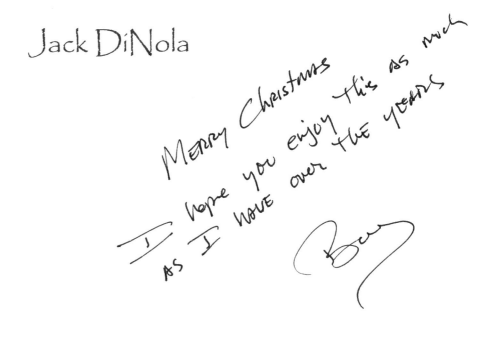

Merry Christmas
I hope you enjoy this as much
as I have over the years

Ben

Abbott Press books may be ordered through booksellers or by contacting:

Abbott Press
1663 Liberty Drive
Bloomington, IN 47403
www.abbottpress.com
Phone: 1-866-697-5310

Because of the dynamic nature of the Internet, any web addresses or links contained in this book may have changed since publication and may no longer be valid. The views expressed in this work are solely those of the author and do not necessarily reflect the views of the publisher, and the publisher hereby disclaims any responsibility for them.

Any people depicted in stock imagery provided by Thinkstock are models, and such images are being used for illustrative purposes only.

Certain stock imagery © Thinkstock.

ISBN: 978-1-4582-1236-8(sc)
ISBN: 978-1-4582-1237-5 (hc)
ISBN: 978-1-4582-1235-1 (e)

Printed in the United States of America.

Abbott Press rev. date: 11/19/2013

abbott press®
A DIVISION OF WRITER'S DIGEST

About the Author:

Jack DiNola was born from immigrant parents in 1917 in Trenton NJ, went to Trenton High School and put himself through Rutgers University, at night, to become an attorney at law practicing in NJ and qualified to practice in front of the Supreme Court. He served in both WW II and the Korean conflict in the Army. When he left the service to finish his college education he had achieved the rank of Lieutenant Colonel, although he never retired from the Army. During his service he was awarded a Bronze Star with two Oak Leaves, a 1st Combat Infantry Badge, a Purple Heart and many other military awards. Enjoy many other poems by Jack in the book "Poems about Love, War and Just for Fun".

Approximately 1950.

Photo December 1964
The DiNola's, Jack, Ethel, Diane and Barry

This is a dedication to the memory of Jack and Ethel from Barry and Diane.

A portion of any proceeds from the sale of this book will be donated to children with diabetes.

We want to thank you for taking the time to read this book and hope you enjoy it as much as we have over the years.

Written by: Jack DiNola
Created by: Barry DiNola
Illustrated by: Barry DiNola
                Nicole Lee

2

Dedication

This is dedicated to the memory of our father Jack DiNola and our mother, his wife, Ethel M. DiNola from Jon Barry DiNola & Diane L. DiNola.

Jack DiNola, son of Mathew DiNola and Theresa (Chiavetti) DiNola, born October 1917, died March 18, 1969. Ethel May DiNola, daughter of Emelia and Ernest Dreher, was born February 12, 1919 and died December 17, 1967.

This poem was written by Jack DiNola, in 1952, who started writing as a young man up until his death. "Two Squirrels and a Mouse" was written while Jack was serving in Korea during the Korean conflict to his children Barry and Diane. The complete works by Jack are available in a poem book called *"Poems about Love, War, and Just for Fun"* which contains 174 poems. Jack started writing poetry as early as the 9th grade and possibly earlier we don't know for sure. Poetry was a small hobby of our father's and while he was alive he sponsored a poetry contest (with

Barry at age 4.

a cash prize) each year at Ewing High School. For a number of years we kept it going after his death, until the school stopped due to lack of interest. He would write on a napkin while having lunch or dinner someplace or whenever something influenced him. As one reads "Poems About Love, War and Just for Fun" it is obvious many were written during war time, about dying or death, that's because Jack served in WWII in Europe and in the Korean conflict. Some were written while on board ship traveling to and from these wars others while stationed in some foreign country. He was a Lieutenant Colonel when he left the service to complete his law degree at Rutgers University and had been awarded a bronze star with two Oak Leaves, a 1st Combat Infantry Badge, a Purple Heart and many other military awards while serving. What I do know and remember about him is that he was a true patriot, he loved this country.

Barry

My dad was in Seoul, Korea fighting in the Korean Conflict. During his assignment there he took time to write a Christmas story for my brother Barry and me. I was 5 or 6 years old and my brother was 2 years younger.

Diane at age 6

The story was than recorded on a record along with a message to my mom, Barry and I. It was first played at Christmas time one evening, my dad still in Korea. I remember sitting on the step that led into our living room, my mother was sitting in a chair in front of me, and the lights from our Christmas tree were the only lighting in the room. I'm sure my brother was there along with my grandmother who lived with us but I don't recall just where they were. When the record began playing I heard my daddy's voice saying: "hello..." I burst into tears and ran to my room sobbing. It was a long time before I could listen to that recording, and not cry. I still choke up when reading the poem to my grandchildren and others during the holidays. The message in the story is even more relevant today, and its sweetness is timeless. I hope you will share this story for years to come and pass it on to those you love. Know that the children for which it was written will delight in knowing that their dad's memory will go on forever. Merry Christmas to you all!

Diane

A portion of any proceeds received from the sales of this book will be donated to the Children with Diabetes.

Two Squirrels and a Mouse
A Christmas Story

by
Jack DiNola

Designed & Created by
Jon Barry DiNola

Illustrated by
Jon Barry DiNola
Nicole D. Lee

Shall I tell you little children
About one Christmas night,
When snowflakes gently covered
All the things that lay in sight.

When the rooftops wore a blanket
That was made with flakes of snow,
And the trees were holding hands
While swaying to and fro

There down beneath some forest tree
There was a little house.
And in it lived some creatures
Four squirrels and a tiny mouse.

The squirrels were making cookies
Out of acorns, roots and leaves,
And the little mouse was trembling
Because he was afraid he'd sneeze.

For if he sneezed out loud he knew
The squirrels would make him go
And spend his Christmas night
In the forest in the snow.

So with his little fingers
He held onto his nose
And prayed with all his tiny might
That the sneeze away would go.

He held his moist pink nosey
Until he thought he'd burst,
And then it suddenly went
KER CHOO-KER RICK-KER CHURST.

What a horrible racket
Resounded through the house,
And Mommy and Daddy squirrel said
"That sounds just like a mouse."

So with bushy tails they scurried,
Searching in pots and pans,
Until they found him hiding
Beneath his trembling hands.

Oh, the little mouse was frightened
Wondering what they'd do
When they found his hiding place
Next to the wooden shoe.

Mommy and Daddy squirrel just laughed
As they saw him hiding there,
Because his bottom was showing
And it was cold and bare.

"Now what shall we do with him", they said,
As they looked at his surprise,
"Shall we give him a pair of panties
Or give him a piece of pie?"

When the mousey heard them whisper
About delicious pie,
He quickly dropped his fingers
That were covering his great big eyes.

The light that shown from the lantern
Made him blink like a little owl
So Mommy and Daddy called him Blinky,
and oh how the children howled.

"Come into the kitchen, they said,
And we'll watch Mommy bake.
You can even help us shell
The acorns for our cake.

For tonight it will be Christmas
And Santa's on his way,
And when he comes with all our toys
We'll all get up and play."

But Mommy and Daddy heard them,
As they plotted their little scheme,
And tucked them all in a leafy bunk
So they could rest and dream.

So Blinky and the little squirrels
Their names were Blushy and Pluck
Settled themselves in dreamland
And wished St. Nicholas luck.

With their tails the three were cuddled
In a bed made up of leaves,
And not a sound was whispered,
Not even a tiny sneeze.

So Mommy and Daddy squirrel
Adopted Blinky mouse
Then decorated the Christmas tree
And the fireplace in the house.

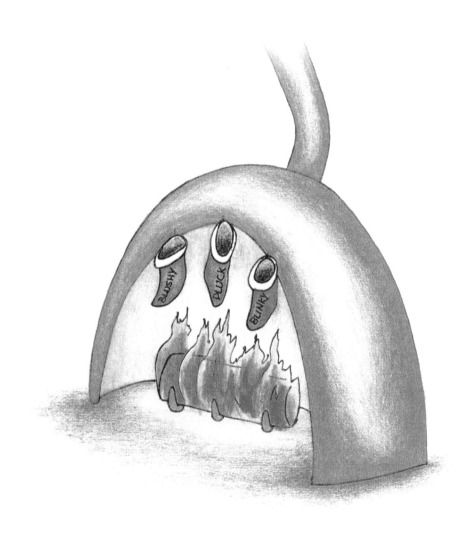

They hung three little stockings
By the chimney-stack with care,
Put a log upon the fire
And some pie beside the chair.

For Santa would be tired
And there he'd sit awhile,
He'd smoke his briar pipe
As he'd watch the children smile.

And then he'd fill their stockings
With fruits and nuts and toys,
And his twinkling eyes would sparkle
As he pictured them filled with joy.

So off to bed traipsed Mommy
And Daddy followed behind,
Everything was quiet, except
The wooden stairs they climbed.

They squeaked with a terrible racket
So they tiptoed up instead,
And lazily put their 'jamas on
And crawled into their bed.

Soon everything was quiet,
Even the fireplace slept,
Until there came a tinkling
'Twas Santa on his sled.

Down the tree he scampered
And quickly entered the house,
Leaving a lot of presents
For Blushy, Pluck and mouse.

He gobbled up his snack
Of milk and apple pie,
Then pulled on his ear to signal
Twas time for him to fly.

Off he went with his bundles
To visit his forest friends,
And leave them Christmas packages
It seemed there'd be no end.

Well, Blushy, Pluck and Blinky
Sleeping soundly as can be,
Never heard St. Nicholas
Go up the houselike tree.

Off he went in the moonlight,
On the wings of a big ole bird,
To leave nice gifts for forest friends
All over this whole world.

Blushy and Pluck and Blinky
Awoke a short time later,
And never in all the woodland
Was there ever such a clatter.

As from their bunks they scrambled
And in wondrous surprise,
Saw so many presents
Right there before their eyes.

Stockings were filled with candy
And goodies and clothes and things,
And even a couple of books
With songs that they could sing.

So Blushy and Pluck and Blinky
Started singing with all their might
And the song they chose to sing
Was the one called "Silent Night".

Two squirrels and a mouse were singing
In front of the fireplace
They sang so very rapidly
You might think it was a race

The loudest of all was Blinky,
He was singing loud and clear,
"MERRY CHRISTMAS EVERYBODY, MERRY
CHRISTMAS AND MAY YOU ALL HAVE
CHRISTMAS CHEER."